Fourteen Slopes

Fourteen Slopes

Mariah K. Hamang

Press

99% Press,

an imprint of Lasavia Publishing Ltd.

Auckland, New Zealand

www.lasaviapublishing.com

© Poems: Mariah K. Hamang, 2021

Cover/Design: Daniela Gast

Photo of the Author by Julia Totino

ISBN: 978-0-9951398-4-8

To Istanbul

Contents

smash, on mute   7

may   10

stasis, illness   12

multi   15

the crevice   18

for now   20

aptitude   23

doorstep   25

quarry   28

triggers   30

accompaniment   33

groundwater   35

thumbing   37

restrictive   40

the pyres   44

mother may i?   46

early march   49

truly   50

landslide   52

desolate   54

dare   55

smash, on mute

like the beginning of any good thing

                      i feel coming up

from within me a plan i didn't know i had

it involves me imagining the space between us

as a canvas where i spell out every instability

already leaking through my teeth, separating

plaque congealed in browning little hollows

                  of my dormant gum line

i begin forgetting to tidy up every inch

of this dinner conversation

invaded by the realization that there are

          air pockets and nitrogen and sunlight

          trapped in my cheekbones, in my fiber

                      eating at my side of

               our intersubjective call & response

                      out it slips from the tension

                      an impulse, seconds before

i remember this never works out

    this dipping into lusty unpredictable rampage

how many examples must i offer up to the heavens

or up to myself, for that matter

                              to remember to leave it be?

i ought to remember to clean up my act

keep my eyes on my own paper

    my blood in my own veins

the problem wasn't confusion my whole life

it was just not knowing. it's just not

                    something to solve.

supports made of cord, and plastic or whatever

and layers, like a story, or even just the past couple days

everything becomes contaminated, even

granite. the pale, pink ash smudged on his face, staring

at his car on the bed of a tow truck

    and it's just some tuesday, it's just someone

having a bad day

dealing with the aftermath of someone else's

resolution, a ripple through the calm as though

it were the shrilling bleat of chaos

as though it were our hands whimpering from

shame more generally reserved for our sex organs

everywhere there is sweat we are suspicious now

we only compromise so that i can silently measure myself

a larger margin of distortion until

we lock into the accidental stalemate.

i am terrified to touch your stomach

i am dreaming so hard of the dishwater

of turning off the television

of sweeping all the hair that falls

and comes

and falls again

may

a string of pale graspings

the furthest thing from coincidence

      recent transformations again in flux

      you suddenly like sports, men

the pieces that travel the world with you are

carried around through hillside and horizon

down hillside and horizon they roll.

      past errors and familiar compost

      recycled—tribal, adherent

unchallenged abdomens locked in a vine of

romances, a sprout popping every night

a shout. a hard prick, menstruation—

some things are simple.

      gridlocked head-to-head with your convictions

      your unrewarded behaviors

      false but comprehensible sentences

meaningful faces

      blindness soldered through the eyebrows

      blindness made gold by the pulp. stripes

speculative biceps, budding molds

terrible thunderstorms

your words sautéed in butter

stasis, illness

life picks up. out from

    the bleak few days

    periodic grumblings

low-level registers of bleeding

in a new house for the first time.

i had always expected the worst

        for hours on end

    because i was the only one

    doing any expecting at all.

tearing the pump from the well

dry and wet and indifferent, although

      not as indifferent as i say

    the night chilled too much

    for summer, the rain

    had dropped the cure

i can peel away. i can wander

i can sit here for seconds

      go upstairs for the toilets

go downstairs for the toilet

ask myself again what i am doing

on this floor at all. sea level

mingling up, angling down

trembling with honesty

and injustice and a solid

acceptance that we don't understand

we won't understand

we will forget the lessons

and the consonants and remember

only the feeling, the sliding

the hug of a warmed-over carcass

pretending to practice being alone

falling in love with a symptom instead

the first moments, the stomping of

heartbeats and so many chests

rising and falling

thinking "be careful," palms spread open,

i am not being careful at all.

i am pieced together with clothespins

and blades and alcohol

and the stitches of a terrible hunger

i am talking to strangers

and finding them perfectly average

disinterested. fun to dance with

    difficult to say goodbye to

attractive proposals seldom fulfilled

                chasing myself back to

the starting line, a collection of

ways to abscond with my treasures

    after laying them bare

    after gripping and loosening

the despicable sadness of every conclusion

multi

they cannot all be everyone

you cannot have it all ways

you cannot move to the old world and

expect to not live in the old world

      little fires at the ends of bigger fires

      the exotic to commonplace blurring

seemingly unnoticeable from one side of the code

         from one point of sale to the next

   denim on denim, your hands

   filthy from the dust of ancient castles

   full of the fragrances of island flowers

   grapevines, olive trees, palm leaves

   faintly, the harbor, the north

the reflections. sentences become easier

      you can drop cigarette butts

      at the feet of Byzantine bricks

      the crumbling edges, the dungeons

      full of knucklebones and replicas

      and the ways you are annoyed with yourself

the lifetimes of discontent, trying

to piece together a frankenstein from

half-forms of people, of human beings

who are real and who are only sometimes

the people you want them to be

for a moment, you forget that

things like fortune-telling existed

in shipwrecks and pins and needles

and poor judgment. all the world over

you can cut ties and make ties, or

seek lovers or small talk or genitals

fusion. we all can make eyes

we all can ignore

we all can wear down the paths

with our own foot traffic

the divots in the stairs becoming craters

legs cramping like a sickness in the night

the climate control both a blessing and a confusion

you cannot always be the exception

you cannot always have what you need

you cannot always take the photos

you saw in your mind or with

your own eyes or their small scratches

green pomegranates getting bigger overhead

the angle of the mountains from inside the walls

the tops of the houses over that way—just a memory

distant now, like an old life

or a false address. the things we almost lose

are almost always rectangles, always important

showing up with hope at some front office

with grey signs selling tickets or

an old hotel room in the dark

the trust falls off, builds up

shakes around somewhere near relief

drink by day, tan by day, decide by day

do everything by day

the rose bushes lose color by night

the crevice

the canyon, and valley

all the negative space—

not so striated, nor timeless

what seems like truth

is more of a misspelling

adrenaline fails to interpret motive

we strike up glances

kiss each other's backs

it is tender, but it is also parallel

disorder, in tandem

personal non-descript dishevelments

welcome the damp solidarity

both quiet and loud

panting at a rhythm

that the other hardly hears

the ivory arms and

the tales of accountants, sadly texting you

on thursday afternoon

you could use the silence

you'd rather have the silence

it gets diluted

the power of suggestion, the kidneys

the extension of yourself to your colostomy

you become as fond of its boundaries

as of any other appendage

it is rather like the regular repressed bitterness

you feel at having had a body, anyway

and then the violence

and the smokescreens and

the terrible ways we say good-bye

confining ourselves to hope

that all the love and pain remains somewhere

for us to examine later

never could the heavens be so cruel, so unrelenting

for now

all day, the rooster crowing

every hour, dawn, another dawn

where the child hasn't slept at all

    cried through the night at

the ethnic cacophony of drums

that rumor says were once melodic

 the neighbors upstairs laugh

 swallow their laughter

clink a wine glass at 4 a.m.

and make love sitting up. like us

they cannot predict the future

but they can feel it coming like

a season they'd rather ignore

     if they could

you come back to a mess

    the silverware in disarray

    your sacrifices everywhere in vain

    looking in the face of a man

who never asked you to change

but who changed you anyway

"no, i don't do that anymore"

"yes, i am jealous" yes, i am tempted

by your dropping of terrible hints

by your gummy threats to leave.

the burden of wishing for

bones in your body that never were

these sounds mean something else

to me, this box has a different set of

vocabularies and antiquities

there is still a sweetness about it

but it tastes of a mixture of salt

and maybe something i can't place

like fear, or uncertainty—no

—definitely uncertainty

but all along the palate

there is still you, and the others, and

the arrangements I've made with fate

to always be the one less hurt

soon, though, the game will be up

       and i will go blind with

       the wet burning karma dealt me

   the round red scabs

   of drunken self-sabotage

   on my thighs. at times

i will be motivated solely by

vengeance, by the lullaby

of remaining unmotivated, by

       the depths of my desire

to cease breathing. in a one-bedroom

apartment in a plain residential area

   of a grand and seething city

i will fill the top of every bottle with

the compliments of a new stranger

with the shattered superficiality of

       their cheap offerings

hanging up my picture frames alone

       wishing for a screwdriver

aptitude

                          leave it to god

lay stretched out on your back

looking at the ceiling with a man

getting high. there is nothing to do.

it has been this way for years

for centuries

                          for time immemorial

we pantomime, talk about motorcycles

watch each other clip each other's toenails

               god has no gender. we could debate

     the reasons and

ways we give thanks, but

                is that really a good use of our time?

     haven't you already unplugged

anything at all? how meticulous i could be

if i had thumbs instead of wings!

and talons where i ought to put up

well-manicured cuticle beds. well,

          i lay that to rest.

i offer my integrity as collateral. i will sell out

every blade of grass in this goddamn city

if it means i can wake up before you

doorstep

let it slip through the cracks

stretch out your arm long

                          further

        for optimal effect

don't trip

        don't dig shovels into

        a look of indigestion

           consternation

        you will again arrive at

the conflict, scraping behind

                both your eyelids

    he asks if i am satisfaction

                    i have conjured

        everything from within me

i am giving away little bits of myself

in small barters and fake covenants and

        subverted identity crises

letting how many parts die

standing back to watch them

wither, in pangs of nostalgia for

the burning of witches—

the ones paid for their services

the most valuable, of course

to shatter the earth in a fracture

deep as the hypocrisy

this right here

we are telling the truth like this:

i made you promise to stay

because i know i won't

i must discover investments

i must leave every stone alone

i couldn't make peace with this if i tried

i can't find it in me

to forgive the somber trance of escaping

ending up in the same room

the same mood

but more tired

another type of yawn to count

another near-catastrophe

    a raw throat, a shallow deal

"i just want to make you feel good"

                  and didn't

  and didn't even try for me in practice

  in the perfect absence of demonstration

  in the small aches that the clutter brings

and the blood vessels of memories

your head uncovered in an alleyway

             or a corner store

             or anywhere really

   wherever you are, you are inescapably sentient

you should have never taken men

        in the first place

you should have never been so eager

for love, brushing so close

       so innocently

   with abandonment

only a few steps away each time

from dislocating your shoulder

quarry

The same kinds of hills on the horizon that made you need to start painting, the kind of man who drops his crumbs into the ashtray instead of his stomach. The smells of different countrysides aren't that different—manure, campfire, dust. Near the mosque, the restaurants, near the restaurants, the garbage dump, the holy and the profane gathered together on the same streets, united by stories of broken concrete, jagged sickened windowpanes, obsolete electric lines, plumbing. Sticking out our hands to beg, to pray, to forfeit.

I confess I cannot be myself when we are not speaking. For the first time you laid back and conceded how good I'd made you feel. Then emerged the smell of evergreen, fresh nuts, sea salt, mint. Off the highway, we drove through farrow fields, lemon tree orchards, broken brick huts with roofs of broken clay shingles in villages that will later be ravaged by war—as before, and again, but not yet. Now they look simply like old terracotta, as old as the outskirts of Bursa itself. We roll over, we labor on the exhale of tension, traveler's tension from the winding incompatibilities, the incommunicable tastes, the boiling desire to go separate ways. The stones here remind you of something, the goats here remind you of something, the trees here remind you of something. Tractors and road signs and lumber—the piles of dirt we won't play in. Rusted satellite dishes, raw slabs of marble, eight-year-old boys hitching rides up to their homes in the hillsides. Resting places of the long-forgotten dead, hiding in browns and such colors like white and grey from the sun.

Instead of discussing our irritants, we sat stolid, we never felt bad about looking each other in the eyes and lying. Even something as small as a hummingbird can live five years. And snail shells—I was so afraid to step on snails. Whether they were big and juicy or small and delicate, they were fragile and always crunched between your toes or under your shoes. We stood in the sunset and took one bite too many, shining ourselves with the rays of old suns. Every night I forgive you for the day, things you didn't say, things you did that I imagine. At nighttime, you are a salve to your own gravel, a fresh pomegranate, a bar of chocolate. You said to me with your eyes what you couldn't with your words, and you came up from behind the clouds to shadow the road rash. From there, down on the highway, there were so many fruit stands—bumpy melons, dirty apples: we couldn't believe how close we were to November. We didn't have to pick lanes, we didn't have to split beds, we didn't have to succeed. We didn't have to determine the point of arrival.

triggers

twenty-four years and

i still can't wrap my head around

the idea of god, how everyone here says

to wash your face after everything

like crying or sleeping or sex, and

why can't i stay some place for anyone just once?

devotion is the constant hurt of

savage guesswork

severe commitments—

being so much uglier now

and oh, how we could leave

let me be the worse person

let me hang from the ceiling fan

i want this

i want nothing

i want to vomit all over you

the trees won't grow around you anymore

the smell of paint sticks inside you

nice fresh women for you anywhere.

"i want to be everything"

and in that wish i knew i loved you

our confessions were more sober

the third time around, the third one i loved

yours ignored, in sight

so you could keep me, seize me

think of the glass jar i never came from

the drumbeat of your prejudice

my boots matching his

the laces breaking, disgusting

me having fallen now beneath the worst I could do

trampled in towers of my fragile complexion

false courtesies, second chances

and the most terrible of all—the frostbitten ideal

that turns black and flakes off all at once

that recovers nothing

that hides like everyone behind their own teeth.

your smiles were so handsome

i don't know who you are anymore

but i think i love you even now

gangly and desperate and smiling that smile

the face it sits in

the hands it touches

the toes it stubs—i am conflicted

    the impossible rebellion of giving in

                it's all normal

        it's the oldest thing we have

        so we will keep it

accompaniment

the uphill went on forever

every step like sandpaper

webs of lightning cracking

sending chills throughout the park

the cruelest time to celebrate: in the middle

of a rainstorm

half-thoughts, half-waking

declining, the descent of shallow breaths

and flares singing songs of

casual violence in the distance

you chose to touch me only at the times

when you were angry, and the fragments—

i am so tired

of the fragments

the relative efforts, the stiff absence of

compensation

rot. my

slack-jawed reluctance to examine

                        tangled in all the unendable endings

the shine of the fate was relentless

groundwater

i amputated limbs. i pasted sequins on the sockets exposed

began to appear more in myself. in my head, there was drowning

or dripping, a motivation with no room to dry out

always soaking. clicking, whirring, melting down

i was my own technology. i understood myself by seeing

nothing in myself in others. i learned by sheer force of will

by the poor espresso of observation, a flower just steps away

from the wall. i raised my arms in the shape of a tulip.

already overheated, i prayed weak prayers for dehydration

determined the science of sleeping while awake—

narcoleptic dinner conversation, selfish pursuits of the moon.

i swam out to where the names for things come from—

mural, mosaic, the archives of time, how effortlessly

no one noticed the moment you stopped feeling lucky to have me.

it was never the thighs that got tired, or the middle

but the extremities, they worked around, down the flab

down the insults avoiding calamity like a tempted vegetarian.

you were bold, but i was bolder—bold enough to slough you off

and welcome you back in an embrace that scratched like velcro

let you congeal like mesh gripping to my steel follicles

admitting i was first and i was best and you'd always needed me

and please keep pounding out the problems and ironing out the lint

until we have absolutely saturated every possible exit with our

sorry moans and our angry shrieks and our fits of reckless lunacy.

thumbing

how dare she put you through it?

        this isn't rhetoric

this is the actual give and take of life itself

everyone could manage a war

everyone likes a little mystery

everyone knows that love is just

a series of apologies i'm tired of making

        what do i want?

        what do i need?

   why aren't you at the intersection?

we all watch our own propaganda

because it always feels right

            after all

   how could you trust love?

   how could you call this disrespect?

   how could you come to believe

     my version of the truth?

the cosmos constantly tells you

"fall in love!" but you can't stay there

the many gifts of the universe lying

at my feet and i trample them

       in the name of discontent

       in the name of liberation

i am concerned with finding

somewhere to be tomorrow

and tonight, it will come like an avalanche

       over me. i will sit and absorb

       and absorb and absorb until

it is leaking out of me like desperation

a helpless plea to be alone for a lifetime

i contracted my muscles so many hours

when i released them, i turned into mush

a bowl of grits, a puddle of atrophy itself

       how far can i fall?

       how far will you follow?

leftover thoughts and dreams and jealousies

will roll over you like lava, boiling in a cup

scratching out your eyes, i will be gone

maybe

maybe this time i will not flake off your skin

but i won't know why

i won't know why i do anything

i won't know why we chose to make it work

beyond a night or two or three

and months in, years in

i would never forget the beginning

i would never forget how we could

chase those first moments to

the grave

restrictive

I was at all times distracted; he was right. Not just the sounds of construction (the pounding and collapsing) but the smells—plaster, insulation molded black, wet paint. At a certain point, you can't just withdraw. You came so far to get here. Or maybe you were dragged, maybe you floated in on some unpredictable, convenient sense of resignation. Always the fiercer one, I was still instigating without even trying, an endless economy of fire alarms and soft eyes and clock towers stopping. Imbalance, chips of long-gone efforts collected in stripped corners from which they will never be swept.

We quietly projected our secrets on the back wall; knowing they were there, we could glance at them if we wanted to, but we never wanted to. We couldn't abandon our preference for naiveté, the honor with which we clung to our values, defended our unimportant opinions, fought back our half-intentional tears. We tried to heal. At even the initial infliction, we tried to heal as we were still ripping.

We didn't want a name. We had friends we didn't want to name, either. Like most other names, therefore, we remained in a dangle that choked harder as we stitched ourselves out. "People have been dying here for all of time," you commented on the cemeteries. "Don't be angry." I wasn't angry. "Don't be sad." My face fell, gulping down my whole throat, phantom feelings from my tonsils reviving, adenoids again like real broccoli. We didn't notice for many months that the story we were writing wasn't a story at all, but a chapter. It was authentic, as a nightmare is authentic, or a dream—blurry, personalized, later forgotten, but as authentic as the other chapters, as much of a new ending as an overlapped beginning.

He grimaced at the cuticles in my mouth, mistook it for hunger. I hid, in the shame, the yellow crusts that hardened where real tissue had once been. I tore away my affection. His discipline was backwash in his disappointment. It transferred well onto notions of possession—abridged versions of jealousy, withheld evidence, sly cocks of the eye, sins of omission. He would say, "Your life is a matter of style I can't make peace with." I never understood, then, why he kept coming back. And he would, but he couldn't. He couldn't fade into reconciliation, couldn't bring himself to push me any further. He noticed shifts in my demeanor that I hadn't even planned, that I couldn't explain away by shifting back, remaining silent, smiling. My mouth was closed then, like a light turned off. I tried to appear stoic, proud, immune, my volition turning to jelly, starting to ooze from my ears. He could see it. We stroked our own lips, smoothed our blonde eyebrows, veered sharply into each other, squinted in the windows of neighboring cars and mimicked their hand gestures—open palms, smacking the air, imagining the mists of spit spraying in support.

Balance restored. There was no masterpiece of stability. The metric conversions still gave us trouble, for example. Ostensibly, however, we sharpened our sympathies with the narrative, with the daily investment of time. On weekends and evenings, we still played upon stages, inundated with regret, and aimless fretting. I was made of materials he could have backhanded in others, sharp fumes that could have made us both swoon if they weren't the adhesive primer sticking our feet to the floor. It wasn't long before my saliva was muddied with the dirt of the person I am not but wish to be, before he left and surfaced out from the coal mines of incompatibility, before we returned to the dust we can't agree if we believe in.

I couldn't accept that it was temporary—the smile on his face as he slept next to me, in my arms draped around him, laced between my legs. Deeply, comfortably at my side, his mouth corners crooked up, more innocent than he was, giving him away as a lover, having enjoyed me but having more than enjoyed me. Behind our sordid eyelids, we dreamt of sleeping with each other again, even so soon between bouts. Confidence was an art we didn't bother with at that time, circling back to moments of heavy-handed presence.

We couldn't help what we were dreaming, couldn't lose weight anymore. "How awful," I thought, "to love without future," but in truth, I had always been awful. I let the wine age too long, uncorked and chilled and reeking a stench of fermented abandon. I never forgot it was there. Behind the blinds drawn tight, the others were naked, too, their vulnerabilities tied forever to their nervous squandering, putzing, touching. Our guts rumbled in unison, our teeth slimed counterintuitively. I hadn't known myself to be such a stickler for informality, but maybe I had. I have been forgetting who I am. I have been wanting to be someone else. I have spent my tolerance for condescension, spilt glasses of alcohol, embraced more stains on the couch and splotches of ourselves in our embarrassments.

Wheels were invented, yes, but where did they take us? Why? Why did our heads crack down the center, split open at the fear of condensation? In the same room, beside each other, was the smell of warm bread, the hearty welcome of a new favorite meal our families never cooked for us, that we learned to prepare for ourselves. We covered only certain aspects— wooden heirlooms underneath Spanish tablecloths, shoulders crisp beneath Cambodian shawls, the true cost beneath Turkish haggling. Our altruism cowered before untold childhoods, untold risks. There was stadium seating for us everywhere— straight-backed, bold, gritting our teeth—sometimes he was hurt more than me.

Usually, however, I seemed to suffer more. You could tell from the movements of my eyes, rolling, widening, darting in the headlights. The evidence was not a myth; I could not condense my appetite to move beyond. I wanted to multiply every current possibility, throw them all on the next platform, expand them like an exponent. I myself became redacted to the power of ten. His ears were ringing now, his lenience sighing from the bottom of his chest, the ease of his answers diminishing with each hazy response. We glazed over. We lit our thousandth cigarette. I cut at my arms like the old times, frozen in a loop I'd occasionally visit, one I hadn't thought I'd see again, but all the time did. I coveted what wasn't. I negated double negatives ad infinitum. He toasted to Mohammad Ali and commented on when my hands would tremor, trembling, worse at the early hours of the morning, after masturbation, after pressing himself on my stomach in shared ecstasy. The footpaths outside remained lighted. Where should we live? Where can we find the nursery? Leaving the cement to harden or inhaling the sting of acetone, we surrendered to narrow self-defeat. I found new purpose in becoming a beast I never promised to become. The attraction that had pulled me in was now an unspoken compromise, the tired knots of obligation. We pretended we hadn't spoiled. We pretended you would find me in others, that nothing was unique.

Dusk falls. I spill around the flow of the crowd, always stomping past the yellow line, toeing to the big reveal. It becomes every day less important how tethered we are to reality, how lucid we are between the delusions, how many times we tell ourselves that good sex is not love. I could cover my head, I could wear my unapologetic tenacity around my neck and swallow my quiet confessions in sleeping whispers, alone in his company. It would not be the same. It would not bring back the others, or a sense of innocence, or the answers that were given me in tongues or that I sussed out from the unconvincing glimpses of identity, orange and grey and the green shade of bite marks, ruptured. I begin to cross streets with my eyes closed, to make my own holidays, to trust the cane curved round my lips, jammed between my gums, to snap incisors, canines, and molars until I have chewed myself out. The mistakes were so carbonated, they couldn't be touched. The lies were so far from premeditated, we died to call them secrets. We were inaudible. We cancelled the renovations. We jumped from the eighth floor. We never slept at night again.

the pyres

on top of

ash piles

stoking

cinders of

every girl

very near

to you

coughing

out

the dregs of

unkempt

secrets

and yeah

maybe

i am not god

maybe

i am not

a gift

to everyone

but maybe

just to

you

only for now

akin to

six

months

of

long

blessings

and then

the aneurysm

that waited

long enough

for you

to crawl

back

into bed

and break

no new ground

mother may i?

her voice through the phone:

"don't be your father"

"don't live in the past"

it was uglier then

forgive them for everything

forgive them for not looking at you when

you touch the soft skin on their neck

and pick out the lint from their hair

and cry. pull on his sweater

pull on his beard

i have wrapped myself up in this

i have carried over yesterday like a remainder

eyes crossed out, limbs fallen against

your poor excuse for everything

yes, we are uneducated

and we like it that way

you would like it, too, i swear

you are forever too old for breast milk

the connection between our mothers

came in the form of dreams—terrible dreams

unshakeable dreams, where the outcome never came.

often, on the hour, in different time zones

we swear by the reactions

we always knew we'd have—ruined.

this time, i wonder if a better year starts with a worse night

drinking wine outside from the bottle

bosporus snow pelting from paradise

lacing your hands behind his back

down low, and kissing begrudgingly

i slipped and slipped but never fell

i woke up with scrapes and swelling

on my fingers, an unaccounted-for ache

in my left arm. stretching made it worse

breathing through it was a test of patience

all i want now is to lie here in peace

sacrifice my lungs to the combat zone

cry less. be numb. stop terrorizing myself

and just be numb. leave

your pocketbook hidden under the kitchen cabinets

i have gone back to saying what i don't mean

i resist the urge to call manipulation "manipulation"

have you gotten as tired as me? have you woken up

        and prayed to just keep sleeping?

        ignore me, ignore me, ignore me—

i need your love like i need to have a body

this skin is so oily, these nail beds so fragile

    the space around your ankles carries

    the biggest share of your annoyance

    tendons somewhere forgotten

eyes landing somewhere difficult

                i was recycled once before

    my first instinct is to let it happen again

the comfort of the familiar

the comfort of the familiar

the comfort of the familiar

    lengthwise, and clockwise

        i always thought you were wrong

        your aspiration seemed limitless

but wasn't. there were so many fissures and dents

        so many ways for the earth to crack

so many people you kept in your life just for flattery

early march

it is taking me a while

i am trying to use

fewer words. to no avail

i am so angry. i am making

decisions that uncannily resemble mistakes:

booking that weekend flight

yelling about the cigarettes

leaving wet towels on the bathroom floor

the mold

i am molding

i am making leaps on a faith i don't have

i got a terrible haircut

i am distinctly unlovable

i am putting the car in reverse and

never looking back. i'm seeing red

i need to be alleviated. artificially heated

my goals are realigning without my consent

i am sitting on a shelf in a medicine cabinet

i am calling home twice a week

as if i had anything decent to report

truly

i don't feel bad about it.

there is a sensation near to guilt

that is not guilt

that surfaces

in a secret still kept

i see now, in my lips closed comfortably

their normal shade of orchid

how much i have learned of the art of silence

the value i hadn't been capable of adopting

and with that, i nursed

the universes inside me that have

no business reflecting outside

before this was to me deception

now it aligns more with tact, discretion

tight-lipped respect for the loose-lipped

physical commentary. the unspoken catastrophe

that is not then catastrophe

i do not mean to mislead you, but

perhaps you'll look around yourself and

still feel misled

    this may have been my doing

behind my dishonorable iron curtain

                    i have shunned myself enough

              i have restrained so many monologues

              i have drawn enough lines in the sand

    to fit in the box—then

agitated at every moment

                    i am done with devil's advocates

              with decisiveness with the answers

                  it is the season again for bug bites

                              long dusks

                        fresh starts

    the moon has not changed, but the sun is brighter

the days still end, whether i am here for them or not

              whether i have honored you or not

    helicopters. the cascade of distance

the singular moment of eruption

                    the long slope up

landslide

it is humbling to deserve heartache.

you couldn't cast a shadow with

the explanation for all the small cuts

on your body, all the ways we were never

lovers, thin roots sapping limited water

i could never stand on two feet again and be happy

emotion. the beast, the catch never caught—

hooked and baited, unanswered

rasping no response to no desire

    no finish to a middle

    busy minds suckling at

the breasts you never wanted

your merit entirely in words

syllables like "could" and "why" and "nev"

  crashing to the floor

  hung from the hours in a day

nothing here to attach my intentions to

everything here to attach my intentions to

smile at me softer, choose another way to

adjust to the same fate

                        can i have it plain?

—even

        even though

            even i am a forbidden fruit

            sealed, the shipwreck

            the lost perfume

desolate

Over the first few days, I become accustomed to certain things, like the temperature I prefer in the shower again, the evaporated anticipation of someone else walking in the doorway, the discomfort of fearing that maybe I never really did mean anything to you. I sit on this fear like a pot on the boil and I steep there for weeks, months, until all my insecurity is soaked up into the backsplash. One minute I feel intolerable, panicked, untethered, and the next, I feel light, accepting, celebrated. There can be no philosophy about it anymore. It becomes packaged away, another leering lifetime inside of me—me!—still staring at the things you left here for me or you or us. There is nothing harder to leave behind than another human being. There is a kicking and a screaming and a temper tantrum to even be the one walking away. I hate myself for doing this, for knowing when it's time to leave. You had no right to be so unfair, and yet, you were still unfair. Responses to hurt cannot usually be contained. Closure became a luxury. Maybe I will wait forever for it, standing in this living room, folding my arms, listening to the cat shriek for you. Too many times before, too many intimacies turning anonymous, too many sad ways your head can amend me into a monster. The capacity to fine tune your memories to a pulp. There became less to share, there became fewer ways we could be there for each other. We sleep alone now, in separate beds, in the same country, for a few months more at least, and somehow alongside the bleak nights is an energetic morning. And even so, I would die this very instant to avoid this route again. My self, in future versions—may she be far less promising.

dare

once upon a time, there was an end to all things

and now we live out the ends of the endings

everything having climaxed generations ago

and today, the dead pasts blindly competing

once, you had a mind that others could peek into

maybe it took months or increments, but then

you would change. the uncontrollable sadness controlled

there was never any reason for emotion—why

it was so strong, why it led us in the wrong direction

i have buckled under the responsibility of being

someone's first love—absolutely not for me

i don't recommend it. we change masks

right in front of each other, strain to hear

the crinkle of summer rain over the cello music

midday, sitting topless with the window open

as a crime against tradition. what will you not tell me?

why can't i ask? what will we start to beg for?

in the disbelief that i was honest, you submerged

your curiosity, suffocated. all the times

you poked your head around the shoulder

out from the niceties we play before dismissal

try to hold on to mercury, whether liquid or planet

and see how young you'll precipitate dementia.

you will snub out every sorrow with

a faster transmission of misery from plant to lung

to blood. i could have never done it without you

but then again, i probably could. the impossible wanting

the vague lapses in effort, the mystery of anger.

squares will tend to draw in other squares—

not a law of physical nature, but a reality

of pushing myself away. how can we drop it?

how can we stop like the shallow end, dive out

from the eggs? you tell me in your own language

that i am understanding, and i understand you.

it is still so easy to be unfaithful, so rewarding

as if every partner were a 10-year sleep

plunge yourself in me, stub the tips of your longest toes

until they are hard, unyielding, calloused

flake me off like bits of skin, wind me down

flip me over. let me lower my eyes to tuesday

sheepishly collecting loves beneath the table

in the cupboard, stuffing my cheeks with mothballs

and arsenic lace. euthanized, having forced myself

into ambivalence, i will call the same numbers

over and over, try the same passwords

falling down to the stupor of a self-induced coma

CPSIA information can be obtained
at www.ICGtesting.com
Printed in the USA
LVHW091116200121
676961LV00006B/739